GEOLOGY

Investigating the Science of the Earth

JEN GREEN

rosen publishing's
rosen
central®

New York

This edition first published in 2013 by:

The Rosen Publishing Group, Inc.
29 East 21st Street
New York, NY 10010

Copyright © 2013 by Brown Bear Books Ltd

Consultant: Don Franceschetti, Ph.D., Distinguished
   Service Professor, Departments of Physics and
   Chemistry, The University of Memphis, Memphis,
   Tennessee

Creative Director: Jeni Child
Picture Researcher: Helen Simm
Illustrators: Darren Awuah,
   Richard Burgess, and Mark Walker
Managing Editor: Tim Harris
Children's Publisher: Anne O'Daly
Production Director: Alastair Gourlay
Editorial Director: Lindsey Lowe

Library of Congress Cataloging-in-Publication Data

Green, Jen.
Geology: investigating the science of the Earth/Jen Green.—1st ed.
p. cm.—(Scientific pathways)
Includes bibliographical references and index.
ISBN 978-1-4488-7200-8 (library binding)
1. Geology—Juvenile literature. I. Title.
QE29.G744 2013
551—dc23

2011047810

Manufactured in the United States of America

CPSIA Compliance Information: Batch #S12YA: For further information, contact Rosen Publishing, New York, New York, at 1-800-237-9932.

CONTENTS

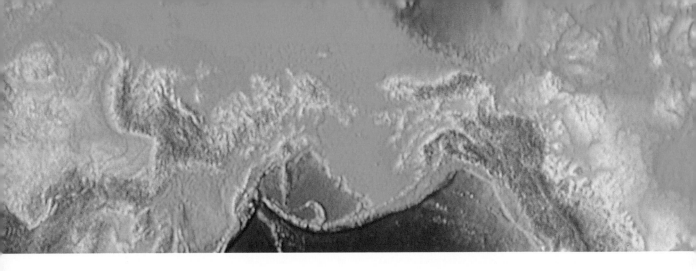

INTRODUCTION

Geology is the study of planet Earth, what it is made of, and how it is shaped. The word geology comes from Greek words that mean "Earth" and "knowledge."

GEOLOGY, AN EARTH SCIENCE, is a vast field of study that covers all the features on and under the planet surface, from the upper atmosphere to the ocean depths. Geologists study continents, landforms, soil, Earth's interior, mountains, islands, oceans, ice, and climate. They examine rocks and minerals to find out about Earth's structure, formation, and history.

Since the dawn of time, people have asked questions about Earth's shape and structure. In ancient times, people wondered about the world that lay beyond the horizon. They thought about whether Earth was flat or round, how old it was, and how it had begun. They tried to figure out what unleashed the destructive power of earthquakes and volcanoes, and how mountains, lakes, and valleys were formed.

Most people now know that Earth is a round, rocky ball—a small planet that orbits the Sun, which is a star like

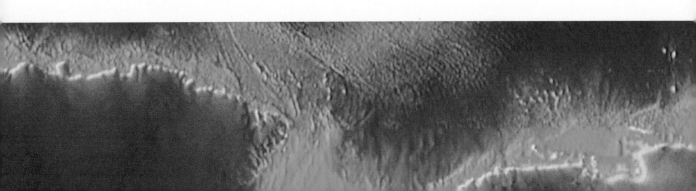

the countless other stars that dot the night sky. Scientists have discovered that Earth is ancient, more than 4.5 billion years old. Rocks can be dated by various methods, including the study of fossils (the remains and traces of once-living things that have turned to stone).

Earth's surface is continually shaped by the forces of wind, ice, and running water. Earth's outer crust is made up of about twenty huge, rigid plates that slowly drift about and jostle. These movements cause earthquakes and volcanic eruptions, and form mountains. Scientists also know quite a lot about the superhot layers of rock that make up Earth's interior, hundreds of miles beneath the crust. Yet just two hundred years ago, many people believed that the center of the planet was filled with water.

All the knowledge about Earth that people today take for granted had to be painstakingly pieced together, often through years of strenuous field work and study. Many ideas, such as the view that Earth is not the center of the universe but instead orbits the Sun, were initially shocking. Some of the scientists who proposed them were ridiculed; a few were threatened with torture. This is the story of how geologists gradually discovered all we now know about planet Earth.

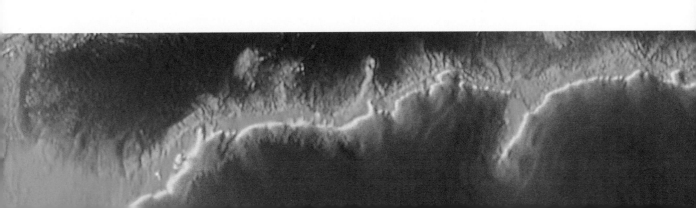

1 IDEAS OF THE ANCIENTS

In ancient times, before anyone understood the structure of Earth, people generally linked the powerful forces of nature with the supernatural. The ancient Greeks were the first to study nature and Earth in the light of reason, not superstition.

ANCIENT PEOPLE HAD ONLY their own observations to go on as they tried to make sense of the world around them. They saw the seemingly solid Earth and the wave-tossed oceans that stretched to the horizon, and believed that the world was flat. They watched the Sun, Moon, and stars move across the sky and concluded that these "celestial bodies" circled

BELIEFS IN ANCIENT EGYPT

The ancient Egyptians were skilled astronomers, architects, and builders. Like many others, they relied on religion to explain Earth's origins. They believed that the world was created when the Sun god Ra separated Geb, the Earth god, from Nut, the sky goddess. They thought that Earth was flat and square under a pyramid-shaped sky.

This Egyptian tomb painting shows Ra standing on Geb, who becomes Earth, and lifting Nut, who becomes the sky. On either side of Ra are Tefnut and Shu, who become the atmosphere.

THE FIRST EARTHQUAKE DETECTOR?

The Chinese kept records of quakes from 780 BCE. In the second century CE, Chinese mathematician and astronomer Chang Heng (78–139 CE) invented the world's first seismometer. His device was sensitive enough to detect earthquakes from a distance. Called the dragon jar (model below), it was a brass jar with eight dragons' heads around the rim. Each head had a brass ball in its mouth. Below each head, around the base of the jar, were eight frogs with open mouths. When the ground shook even slightly, the jar shook. That made a ball drop into a frog's mouth. The dropping ball made a clang, which warned people of the quake.

INDIAN BELIEFS ABOUT EARTHQUAKES

Around two thousand years ago, people in India believed that Earth was balanced on the back of four giant elephants, which in turn stood on a huge turtle, which was balanced on a cobra. People believed that Earth shook whenever any of the animals moved.

constantly, while Earth stood still. Myths (traditional stories) arose to explain how Earth and everything on it came into being. In many different cultures, including ancient Egypt, people believed that the world with all its wonders was the work of gods and goddesses, who had shaped Earth and the heavens and created plants, animals, and humankind.

Less kindly gods were often linked with destructive natural forces such as earthquakes and volcanic eruptions. In many cultures, earthquakes and eruptions were a sign that the gods were angry. In India, people believed that Earth shook because it rested on giant animals. The ancient Chinese had a more practical approach. The world's first earthquake detector was devised

THALES

In the sixth century BCE, the philosopher Thales of Miletus (625–546 BCE; right) suggested that natural rather than supernatural forces were at work when earthquakes and volcanoes struck. He also observed how water helps shape the land: For example, rivers drop sand and mud at their mouths to form deltas. At a time when people generally believed that fossils were the result of magic, Thales correctly guessed that they were the remains of once-living things that had turned to stone.

in the second century CE by a Chinese engineer, Chang Heng.

The civilization of ancient Greece lasted from the ninth to the second century BCE. The ancient Greeks were among the greatest thinkers the world has ever known. They made huge strides in many branches of learning, including mathematics, philosophy, science, and geology. In the sixth century BCE, the philosopher Thales suggested that natural forces, not the gods, were responsible for shaping Earth's surface. Thales believed that earthquakes and eruptions were also natural. His ideas were among the first to help clear the fog of superstition and religion about how Earth was formed.

PYTHAGORAS

Pythagoras (c. 580–500 BCE) concluded that Earth was round after he observed how ships disappeared beyond the horizon, and heard travelers' tales that unfamiliar stars could be seen in the night sky in the far north and south. He believed that Earth was the center point of the universe, around which transparent spheres that carried the Sun, stars, planets, and all other heavenly bodies circled.

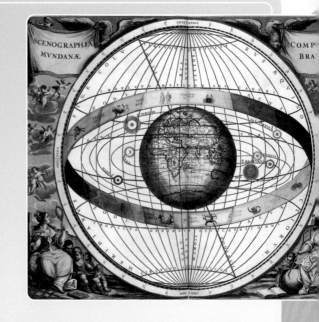

This medieval map of the heavens shows Earth at the center of the universe.

Greek thinkers were among the first to realize that Earth was round, not flat. In the sixth century BCE, the mathematician Pythagoras suggested that Earth was a sphere. Two centuries later, the great philosopher Aristotle listed all the facts that supported Pythagoras's theory. For example, he observed that, during an eclipse, the shadow Earth cast on the Moon was curved, and concluded that Earth must be a sphere and not a flat disk. Both Pythagoras and Aristotle, however, believed that Earth was the center of the universe. They had no idea that Earth was a planet like Venus, Mars, and Jupiter, which we now know orbit the Sun.

ARISTOTLE ON EARTHQUAKES

Aristotle (384–322 BCE) noted that Earth cast a round shadow on the Moon during an eclipse, which suggested that Earth was a sphere. He believed that Earth was a rocky ball that had taken a very long time to reach its present form. Aristotle was also among the first to offer a scientific explanation (one that was not based on superstition) for earthquakes and volcanoes, suggesting that they struck when winds fanned enormous fires that burned inside Earth.

According to Aristotle, hot underground winds occasionally burst forth in volcanic activity and earth tremors. He believed the winds caused rifts (such as this one in California).

ARISTARCHUS OF SAMOS

Aristarchus (c. 310–c. 230 BCE) claimed that the movements of the Sun, Moon, and stars across the sky could be explained by Earth turning on its axis once a day and orbiting (circling) the Sun once a year. Earth's axis is an imaginary line (right, pink) from pole to pole. Aristarchus was right, but no one accepted his ideas for more than a thousand years.

Earth's axis

PLINY THE ELDER

Pliny the Elder (23–79 CE) wrote the 37-volume *Natural History* that detailed all Roman knowledge about rocks, minerals, and fossils. As he observed Mount Vesuvius erupt in southern Italy in 79 CE, Pliny was killed by fumes. The scholar's nephew, Pliny the Younger, became a famous writer. He also watched the eruption and wrote an eyewitness account.

In the third century BCE, a philosopher named Aristarchus of Samos came up with a new idea that threatened to overturn the Greek view of the universe. He suggested that Earth was not the center of the universe, but instead it was a planet that moved around the Sun. Aristarchus was correct, but few people took his ideas seriously at the time.

ERATOSTHENES'S CALCULATION

Eratosthenes (c. 276–c. 194 BCE) knew that at noon in midsummer the Sun cast slight shadows in his home city of Alexandria. He then discovered that to the south in Syene (now Aswan), the Sun shone directly into a deep well at the same time. Thus the angle at which the Sun's rays hit Earth was different in each place. He wondered how that could be if Earth was flat. Eratosthenes got a friend to walk from Alexandria to Syene and measure the distance—roughly 500 miles (800 km). Using that information, the difference in angles of the Sun's rays, and his knowledge of geometry, Eratosthenes figured out that Earth's circumference was 25,000 miles (40,000 km). The true figure is 24,870 miles (40,024 km), so he was amazingly accurate.

By the third century BCE, the Greek city of Alexandria in Egypt had become an important center of learning. An astronomer named Eratosthenes, head of the great library in Alexandria, estimated Earth's circumference using geometry.

Around 250 BCE, the Romans conquered the Greek world. They adopted Greek ideas about geology and added new information on minerals and mining drawn from every part of the huge Roman empire. In the first century CE, the Roman writers Seneca and Pliny the Elder produced major works on geology. By the second century CE, Greek scholar Strabo as well as Ptolemy, another great Alexandrian scholar, had produced important multivolume works on geography. The work of both remained important for centuries.

EARLY WORKS ON GEOGRAPHY

Around two thousand years ago Greek geographer and historian Strabo (c. 64 BCE–23 CE) produced the most detailed review of geographical knowledge then available. His seventeen-volume *Geography* discussed the aims and methods of geography, described known regions, and reviewed earlier writings. All that is known about the work of many early geographers comes largely from Strabo's reviews. Ptolemy (c. 100–170 CE) produced the eight-volume *Guide to Geography*. It discussed geographical principles and how to draw maps. Most important were Ptolemy's invention of lines of latitude and longitude.

Lines of longitude (right, pink) are every 10 degrees east and west of the meridian (red), an imaginary line that encircles Earth from pole to pole. Lines of latitude (blue) are every 10 degrees north and south of the equator, an imaginary line around Earth's middle. Lines of latitude and longitude allow any place on Earth to be located with accuracy. On this globe, a location 40 degrees north, 30 degrees west is marked.

equator

meridian

point located at 40° N, 30° W

40°

30°

2 THE REBIRTH OF SCIENTIFIC THOUGHT

When the Roman Empire fell in the fifth century CE, Europe entered the Middle Ages, when Greek and Roman knowledge was mostly forgotten. Earth science hardly progressed in Europe for about a thousand years.

IN 391 CE A CHRISTIAN MOB wrecked Alexandria and burned the works of the Greek philosophers. Ancient knowledge of Earth was lost for hundreds of years. Many people, even learned scholars, went back to believing that the world was flat. Medieval maps showed Earth as

This painting from 1530 shows God, Adam, Eve, and animals in the Garden of Eden.

THE BIBLICAL CREATION STORY

The Old Testament tells how God created Earth in six days by dividing light from darkness, dividing the land from the waters, and creating plants, animals, and people. The story also tells how God later punished human wickedness by sending a flood that drowned every creature except those aboard Noah's ark. These two stories influenced Christian, Muslim, and Jewish ideas about Earth's origins for thousands of years. All three religions share stories that appear in the Old Testament.

AVICENNA

In the 1020s Arab scholar Avicenna (980–1037 CE; right) wrote books about natural science in which he drew on Greek learning and added his own ideas on the origins of rocks and mountains. Avicenna understood that the moving water of rivers and oceans helps shape the landscape. He went astray, however, in his understanding of fossils. Like many people of his day, he thought that fossils were the result of unsuccessful attempts by Earth itself to create living things.

a flat disk, with the lands of the known world in the center, surrounded by ocean. The biblical stories of Creation and the Flood were used to explain Earth's origins.

Beyond the borders of Christian Europe, Greek learning, including Ptolemy's great works, survived in Arabic translation. Muslim scholars such as Avicenna added their own observations. Beginning in the late fourteenth century, the Renaissance saw the revival of classical learning in Europe, and the start of a new interest in science and geology. In 1395 Ptolemy's *Guide to Geography* was translated from Arabic. Renaissance figures, such as the Italian artist Leonardo da Vinci, tried to find out more about the natural world.

LEONARDO DA VINCI

The famous Italian artist and inventor Leonardo da Vinci (1452–1519; left) was keenly interested in earth science. He knew that fossilized seashells were found high on mountains. The Christian Church said that they had been washed there by the biblical flood, but Leonardo guessed correctly that the rocks that contained the ancient shells had once been under water.

The Renaissance was the great age of European exploration, when knowledge of the world changed quickly. In 1492 Italian navigator Christopher Columbus landed on the shores of America—the "New World." In 1522 Portuguese explorer Ferdinand Magellan sailed around the world, which finally proved that Earth was a sphere. These and other discoveries sparked new interest in geography, geology, and mapmaking.

The sixteenth century brought new discoveries in earth science. In 1530 Polish astronomer Nicolaus Copernicus claimed, like Aristarchus, that Earth was a planet that revolved around the Sun. Around 1540 a German mining expert named

ADVANCES IN MAPMAKING

In the 1550s Dutch geographer Gerardus Mercator (1512–1594) devised a new method of showing Earth's curved surface on a flat map. The method, called Mercator's projection (an eighteenth-century example below), works by stretching the areas around the poles to make spherical Earth into a cylinder. This makes lands farther away from the equator appear bigger than they really are.

FATHER OF MINERALOGY

Agricola (1494–1555 CE) was among the first people to base a natural science on observation, not on speculation. In his book *De re metallica*, he described mining and smelting. His book *De natura fossilium* has the first scientific classification of minerals, based on their properties, and describes many new minerals. This was the first mineralogy textbook. It earned Agricola the title "father of mineralogy."

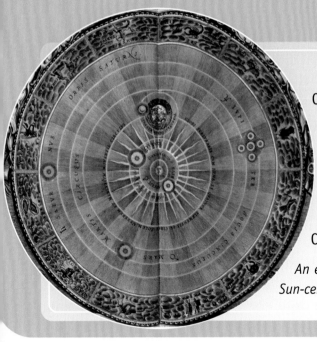

COPERNICUS

Copernicus (1473–1543) was a Polish priest with a passion for astronomy. In his day, people believed Earth was the center of the universe. Copernicus realized that this did not fit with astronomers' observations. His idea of Earth as a planet revolving around the Sun contradicted Christian teaching. Copernicus's book was banned by the church.

An eighteenth-century illustration of Copernicus's Sun-centered solar system.

Georgius Agricola wrote important new works on geology, mining, and metals. In the late 1500s English doctor William Gilbert showed that Earth was a giant magnet, which is why compasses point north.

New world maps that showed the Americas were printed. This allowed English philosopher Francis Bacon (1561–1626) to notice that the coastlines of South America and Africa looked as if they had once fitted together. This suggested they had once been joined, but the theory of plate tectonics (see page 35), which explained Bacon's observation, did not emerge for another three hundred years.

EARTH AS A MAGNET

William Gilbert (1544–1603), doctor to the English queen Elizabeth I, used magnetized needles to demonstrate that Earth behaves like a giant magnet. Like a huge bar magnet, the planet has two poles, in the far north and south. Scientists now know Earth's magnetic field, called the magnetosphere, extends far into space, where it helps protect the planet from harmful rays from the Sun.

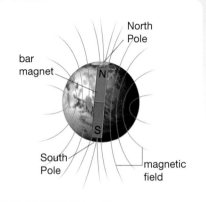

3 THE NEPTUNISTS AND PLUTONISTS

At the start of the seventeenth century, ideas about Earth's origins and structure still had to agree with the church's teachings. Then came the Age of Enlightenment, when scientists took a new, rational approach to old ideas.

IN THE EARLY 1600s ITALIAN astronomer Galileo Galilei used the newly invented telescope to study the Moon, Sun, and planets for the first time. What he saw confirmed Copernicus's view of the universe, but this got Galileo into trouble with the Catholic Church.

GALILEO

In 1632 Galileo Galilei (1564–1642; right, in front of telescope) published a book that confirmed Copernicus's belief that Earth is a planet that orbits the Sun, but the book was quickly banned by the church. Galileo was forced to publicly withdraw his support of Copernicus under threat of torture, but he never really changed his mind. In the field of physics, Galileo carried out experiments that showed falling objects accelerate at the same speed whatever their weight. This discovery helped Isaac Newton develop his laws of motion (*see* page 19).

THOMAS BURNET

English churchman Thomas Burnet (1635–1715) supported the church's view of Earth's origins. He was one of a group of scientists who believed that beneath a thin, rocky crust, Earth's interior was filled with water, like a giant egg. At the time of the Great Flood, people believed that God had released waters from inside Earth to cover the surface. The surging waters had buckled and twisted Earth's outer crust to form mountains and other types of landforms.

ROBERT HOOKE AND THE ROCK CYCLE

English scientist Robert Hooke (1635–1703) believed that Earth's surface was shaped not by a single mighty flood, but by slow natural processes that recurred in endless cycles. This theory, now called the rock cycle (below), was way ahead of its time, and no one took much notice of it for years.

Rocks at the surface (1) are broken down by weathering (the action of wind, heat, and rain) into pieces. They are carried downstream by rivers and deposited in seas (2). As more layers are added, deposits are squeezed and form rock (3). Underlying rocks circulate (4) and some melt far below the surface (5). Some reemerge as molten rock or ash (6) at volcanoes or are pushed up and create new underlying rocks (7).

Throughout the seventeenth century, most Christians believed that Earth's landscapes had been shaped by the biblical flood. This view was supported by scholars such as the English cleric Thomas Burnet. In 1650 Irish archbishop James Ussher (1581–1656) added up all the ages of people mentioned in the Old Testament to figure out that the Great Flood had occurred in 2349 BCE, with the Creation itself in 4004 BCE. This made the Earth less than six thousand years old. Around the same time, however, some scholars, including English scientist Robert Hooke, began to question whether the church's view of Earth's origins was correct.

NICOLAUS STENO

Danish geologist Nicolaus Steno (1638–1686; right) realized that if rocks were formed in horizontal layers, the oldest layers would be at the bottom, with younger rocks on top. Steno called this idea the principle of superposition. Geologists still use Steno's theory to figure out the age of rocks, and in what order rock layers came into existence.

In 1669 Danish geologist Nicolaus Steno made an important discovery. He realized that many rocks were originally deposited in horizontal layers called strata, although natural processes might later twist the layers out of shape. If Steno was correct, Earth's rocky surface had taken a very long time to form, not just a few thousand years as the church suggested. Somewhat later, the flamboyant French naturalist Comte de Buffon conducted experiments that seemed to confirm that Earth was much older than the church claimed.

COMTE DE BUFFON

Like the Plutonists (*see* page 20) Georges Louis Leclerc, Comte de Buffon (1707–1788; right), believed Earth was a white-hot ball that had cooled. He heated some metal balls until they were white-hot, and then timed how long they took to cool. He used the results to calculate that the Earth had taken at least seventy-five thousand years to cool to its present temperature.

In the late seventeenth century the great English physicist Isaac Newton developed his universal laws of gravity. Newton realized that the force of gravity, which causes objects to fall to the ground, also holds the Moon in orbit around Earth and the planets in orbit around the Sun. Newton's work on gravity enabled scientists to figure out Earth's mass (the amount of matter it contains) and volume (see box below): Objects exert a force of gravity on each other. According to Newton's laws, if the masses of two objects are multiplied, the force of gravity is proportional to the result. The force of gravity on lead weights of known mass can be measured. From that measurement, the mass of Earth can be calculated.

NEWTON AND EARTH'S SHAPE

Newton (1643–1727) suggested that Earth's rotation would affect the planet's shape. As Earth turns about its axis (*see* page 10), areas around the equator travel much faster than the poles. This is because the Earth's axis runs through the poles. So areas around the equator travel the full distance of Earth's circumference. But areas around the poles travel only a short distance, as if they were spinning on the spot. Newton believed this effect would distort Earth's spherical shape, causing it to bulge very slightly at the equator and flatten at the poles. This idea was confirmed in the 1960s, when satellites took the first pictures (above) of Earth from space (*see* page 37.) Because scientists know the shape and mass of Earth, they are able to figure out the volume (the amount of space Earth takes up).

In the late eighteenth century, a debate about Earth's interior and formation developed between two groups of scientists, the Neptunists and the Plutonists. The Neptunists believed that Earth's interior was filled with water. They thought that all rocks at the surface had formed as sediment settled on the bed of a great ocean that had once covered Earth. The Plutonists, on the other hand, believed that Earth's interior was molten rock, which erupted onto the surface as volcanoes. They were led by Scottish doctor James Hutton.

THE NEPTUNISTS

The Neptunists were named after Neptune, the Roman god of the sea. They were led by the German geologist Abraham Gottlob Werner (1749–1817; below). Werner and his followers believed that the rocks at Earth's surface had been formed at the time of the Great Flood, and since then very little change had occurred.

JAMES HUTTON AND THE PLUTONISTS

The Plutonists were named for Pluto, the Roman god of the underworld. Their leader, James Hutton (1726–1797; below), believed Earth began as a ball of white-hot rock that had slowly cooled. Plutonists also thought that Earth was gradually shaped by natural forces, including volcanoes and the action of pressure, water, and heat and in processes that were still continuing. Hutton devoted his later life to scientific reading and traveled widely to inspect rocks and observe the actions of natural processes. His theory (called uniformitarianism) was astonishingly accurate. He suggested that vast amounts of time were needed for Earth to form in this way, and so it was much older than previously thought.

HOW ROCKS ARE FORMED

All rocks are now grouped into three types according to how they were formed: igneous, sedimentary, or metamorphic. Igneous rocks form when red-hot molten rock erupted by volcanoes cools. Sedimentary rocks form when sediment (rock fragments) carried by rivers collects in lakes and oceans and is compressed (squashed). Metamorphic rocks form when existing rocks are changed by great heat and pressure inside Earth's crust.

Marble (1) is limestone rock that has been hardened by heat or pressure, so it is a metamorphic rock. Granite (2) is formed by the cooling of molten rocks, so it is an igneous rock. Sandstone (3) is made up of layers of sand-sized grains of rock. It is the second-most common sedimentary rock.

Gradually, European geologists gathered more evidence to support the second theory, which proved correct. In the 1760s French geologist Nicolas Desmarest (1725–1815) studied the rocks of the Auvergne region in central France, and realized that they were volcanic in origin. Another French scientist, Dieudonné Dolomieu (1750–1801), observed an eruption of Mount Vesuvius in Italy—the same volcano that Pliny the Elder and his nephew had witnessed. Dolomieu realized that lava comes from deep inside Earth. At the time, no one thought that volcanoes played a major role in creating rocks at the planet's surface. Now scientists know that volcanic action is one of the three ways in which rocks are formed.

4 NEW THEORIES EMERGE

In the first half of the nineteenth century, geologists began to discuss how mountains formed and the significance of glaciers and fossils. Meanwhile, new discoveries shed light on the old questions of Earth's age, and what lay below the outer crust.

IN THE EARLY 1800s THE DEBATE between the Plutonists and Neptunists continued. Opinion began to favor the Plutonists, who believed that Earth's interior was red-hot molten rock.

Two German geologists, Alexander von Humboldt and Leopold Buch, who had been Neptunists, became Plutonists after they visited the Auvergne in France and Mount Vesuvius in Italy.

ALEXANDER VON HUMBOLDT

German baron Alexander von Humboldt (1769–1859; below) was not only a scientist but also a great traveler who explored the Amazon region of South America. In the course of his travels, he discovered that similar rocks were present on the coasts of eastern South America and West Africa. This supported the idea that the two continents had once been joined (*see* pages 32–33.)

LEOPOLD BUCH

The German geologist Leopold Buch (1774–1853; below) studied geology under the great Neptunist Abraham Werner. Werner and his followers believed that volcanoes burned a fuel like coal, which had been formed through sedimentation as rock fragments settled out of water. When Buch visited the Auvergne, however, he could find no trace of this fuel. Instead he realized that some of the rocks were volcanic in origin, which suggested that the Plutonists were right.

JAMES HALL

James Hall (1761–1832) heated rocks in a large furnace to imitate conditions inside a volcano. He discovered that when limestone (a sedimentary rock) was heated, marble (a metamorphic rock) was formed. A similar experiment with volcanic rocks produced granite, an igneous rock. These experiments supported James Hutton's theory that Earth gradually changed and confirmed ideas about how rocks formed.

Scottish scientist James Hall conducted experiments that involved heating rocks. Hall's results supported Hutton's ideas.

In 1815 an English surveyor named William Smith made an important discovery. He realized that fossils could be used to establish the age of rocks.

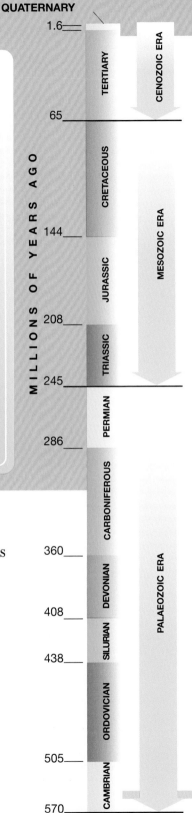

WILLIAM SMITH

William Smith (1769–1839) worked as a surveyor and canal builder. While at work, he noticed that different kinds of fossils occur at various levels in strata (layers) of sedimentary rocks. As he traveled, Smith realized that different types of fossils appear in the same order in rock layers, even if the rocks themselves are different in different areas; for example, if one area contained sandstone, and another chalk. Smith rightly concluded that rocks that contained the same fossils must be the same age.

Modern geologists divide Earth's geological history into eras and periods (left). The dates of eras and periods were originally based on studies of layers and the age of fossils found in rocks. Today, modern dating techniques (see page 31) are used to figure out the ages of rocks.

23

CUVIER AND THE CATASTROPHISTS

Cuvier thought that Earth was formed a relatively short time ago. His work on fossils and geology convinced him that Earth's surface had changed greatly during its existence. Cuvier's work brought new life to the old idea of catastrophism, which was based on theories such as those of the Neptunists (*see* page 20). Cuvier thought the changes in Earth's surface were caused by a series of catastrophes. These included sudden land upheavals caused by earthquakes, as well as floods. Cuvier believed Noah's flood to be the most recent flood.

HOW FOSSILS ARE FORMED

Fossils are the remains or traces of living things that have turned to stone. They often occur in sedimentary rocks. When an animal or plant dies (**1**), its remains are buried under layers of rock or sediment (**2**). The soft parts of the dead animal rot away. Hard parts such as bones or shells may be preserved, as the sediment slowly hardens into rock. Minerals from these rocks gradually replace the hard parts, forming a fossil (**3**). The fossil-bearing rocks might be discovered and the fossils dug up by paleontologists (fossil scientists).

Smith used this method to date rocks and make the first geological maps of England. Similar maps were soon being made of other regions.

In the 1820s French naturalist baron Georges Cuvier (1769–1832) examined fossils found in the rocks around Paris. Like William Smith, he realized that fossils provide important clues about the age of rocks. Cuvier taught at the Natural History Museum in Paris, an important center for geology. He founded the science of paleontology (the study of fossils), and described how fossils are formed. Around this time, the discovery of dinosaur fossils and the bones of other extinct animals generated huge interest in Earth's prehistoric past.

CHARLES LYELL AND THE UNIFORMITARIANS

Charles Lyell (1797–1875) is sometimes called the father of modern geology. Lyell's *Principles of Geology* was based on Hutton's principles of uniformitarianism (*see* page 20). On his travels around Europe, Lyell gathered a great deal of evidence to prove that all features of Earth's surface are produced by physical, chemical, and biological processes that work at uniform (standard) rates. Earth must, therefore, be hundreds of millions of years old because these natural processes work so slowly. The theory of uniformitarianism was widely accepted by the end of the nineteenth century. Until then, however, there was much debate between uniformitarians and catastrophists. Modern geologists accept a mixture of the two theories.

In the 1830s Scottish geologist Charles Lyell published a three-volume work, *Principles of Geology*, which became one of the most important science books of the nineteenth century. Lyell confirmed James Hutton's view that natural forces were continually shaping the land. After this, Hutton's ideas were generally accepted. Around the same time, the Swiss-born naturalist Louis Agassiz discovered that glaciers play an important role in shaping the landscape because they gouge out wide, U-shaped valleys and deposit piles of rock debris called moraine. Agassiz suggested that ice sheets had once covered much of North America and Europe. Many people scoffed at this idea at first, but it was correct.

AGASSIZ AND ICE AGES

By studying the geology of different regions, Swiss American naturalist Louis Agassiz (1807–1873) recognized that glaciers shaped many landscapes that were then free of ice. Agassiz realized that Earth's climate had been much colder at various times in the distant past. During the long, cold periods he called ice ages, ice sheets stretched from the Arctic as far as Europe and the United States. As Earth's climate slowly warmed and cooled, the ice either receded or advanced.

Ice cover in the Arctic today (1) and 1.6 million years ago (2).

25

Around 1850, Irish engineer Robert Mallet (1810–1881) was studying earthquakes and volcanoes when he made a breakthrough. He made a world map that showed the sites of earthquakes and eruptions. The map showed that these mostly occurred in narrow zones that we now know lie on the borders of the giant plates that make up Earth's crust (see page 35.)

Mallet made another important discovery when he found a way to measure the speed of the vibrations (or shock waves) that pass through the ground after an explosion. His work helped found the modern science of seismology. Seismology is the study of Earth's structure using seismic waves (shock waves from earthquakes and volcanoes; see pages 30–31).

PACIFIC OCEAN

EARTHQUAKE AND VOLCANO ZONES

Each year, thousands of earthquakes and smaller tremors strike, and around five hundred volcanoes are active. This geological activity takes place not just anywhere on Earth, but is concentrated along the borders of Earth's tectonic plates (see page 35.) A volcanically active zone called the Ring of Fire runs around the edge of the Pacific Ocean. It corresponds to the rim of the Pacific Plate.

Earth's crust is made up of several plates (see page 35). Earthquakes and volcanoes are common where the edges of these plates meet and put pressure on each other. Around the boundaries of the Pacific Plate are many active volcanoes and frequent earthquakes, shown by red dots on this globe. Earthquakes are more common in this Ring of Fire than volcanic eruptions, and they have caused much damage over the years.

JAMES DWIGHT DANA

Yale University professor James Dwight Dana (1813–1895) was a geologist, mineralogist, and zoologist. He was among those who believed, like the Plutonists, that Earth had begun life as a white-hot ball of rock that had slowly cooled. Dana suggested that mountains had formed during this cooling process, as the outer crust shrank and wrinkled like the skin of a fruit. This idea was called the Shrinking Earth theory, but it was later disproved.

In the mid-nineteenth century geologists started to question how mountains were formed. By then, few scientists supported the old Neptunist idea that waters gushing from Earth's interior during the Great Flood had twisted the crust to form mountains. American geologist James Dwight Dana suggested that mountains had formed as Earth's crust wrinkled like the drying rind of an apple. British geologist George Airy disagreed with this idea, as did American scientist Frank Taylor (1860–1939). Taylor suggested that mountains formed over many millions of years along the edges of continents as the continents pushed against one another (see pages 32–33). This was correct, but people ridiculed Taylor's idea at the time.

GEORGE AIRY

British geophysicist George Airy (1801–1892; left) suggested that the mountains on Earth's crust had roots of rock that were less dense than their surroundings, the mantle (*see* page 30). He maintained that mountains rode on the mantle the way icebergs float in the ocean. Scientists now believe this extraordinary-sounding idea is correct.

DISCOVERING EARTH'S TRUE AGE

In the late nineteenth century, land and sea exploration and the development of new techniques led to fresh discoveries in earth science. In the early twentieth century, German geologist Alfred Wegener came up with the new, startling theory that continents are not fixed, but drift very slowly.

IN THE LATE 1800s SEVERAL nations, including the United States, Britain, and Germany, sent research ships on expeditions to explore the deep oceans. The ships' scientists took soundings to chart the ocean floor and discovered features such as deep trenches and mountain ranges on the

FEATURES OF THE OCEAN FLOOR

Ocean exploration in the late 1800s revealed that the seafloor has landscapes as varied as any on land, with steep cliffs, deep chasms, vast plains, isolated peaks called seamounts, and long mountain chains. On a four-year voyage between 1872 and 1876, the British research ship *Challenger* discovered the Mid-Atlantic Ridge. This feature is part of the mid-ocean ridge, an undersea mountain chain. *Challenger* also found the deepest point in the oceans, the Mariana Trench in the Pacific Ocean.

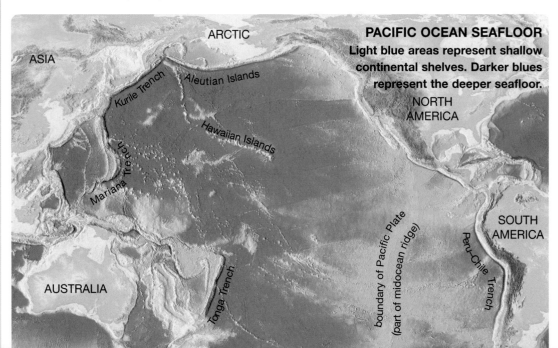

PACIFIC OCEAN SEAFLOOR
Light blue areas represent shallow continental shelves. Darker blues represent the deeper seafloor.

ARCTIC

ASIA

Kurile Trench

Aleutian Islands

Hawaiian Islands

Mariana Trench

NORTH AMERICA

SOUTH AMERICA

boundary of Pacific Plate (part of midocean ridge)

Peru-Chile Trench

Tonga Trench

AUSTRALIA

bottom. They also mapped ocean currents, took water samples, and investigated deep ocean life.

On land, exploration of remote parts of Canada and the western U.S. by geologists such as William Logan, Grove Gilbert, and John Wesley Powell provided Earth scientists with fresh information about rocks, fossils, mountains, and the erosive power of rivers. While he surveyed the Henry Mountains in Utah, Grove Gilbert (1843–1918) came up with a new theory about how mountain ranges had been formed. Gilbert realized that some mountains form as Earth's crust crumples under enormous pressure, in a process now called folding. No one, however, yet understood what had created the forces that could produce pressure of this kind.

WILLIAM LOGAN

Canadian geologist William Logan (1798–1875) explored remote parts of Canada in the nineteenth century. These parts included the Canadian Shield, which is one of Earth's largest continental shields (very large flat regions of a continent). It is centered on Hudson Bay and extends for 3,000,000 square miles (8,000,000 square km) over eastern, central, and northwestern Canada from the Great Lakes to the Canadian Arctic and into Greenland. Logan discovered that the rocks of the Canadian Shield were very ancient.

POWELL AND THE CANYON

John Wesley Powell (1834–1902), who lost an arm fighting in the Civil War, explored the Grand Canyon (below) of the Colorado River in the 1860s by boat and on foot. The work of men like Powell helped geologists see the major role that rivers play in shaping the landscape. Rivers erode (wear away) land and form deep gorges, huge canyons, wide valleys, and lakes.

As the nineteenth century ended, geologists continued to debate what lay beneath Earth's crust. The available data convinced most that Earth's interior was made of several rocky layers, which grew progressively hotter toward the center. They believed that below the solid crust was a layer of softer, semisolid rock called the mantle, which surrounded a superhot core. No one, though, was sure whether the core was solid or liquid. People did not find evidence for their theories about Earth's structure, however, until the seismograph was invented and sophisticated seismographic techniques developed.

In the 1880s British scientist John Milne (1850–1913) invented the seismograph to measure vibrations

SEISMOGRAPHS AND SEISMIC WAVES

At geological stations around the world, seismologists measure seismic waves, created either by earthquakes or artificially by explosions. As the waves pass through the different layers inside Earth—the crust, mantle, and core (*see* page 36)—they speed up or slow down. The waves are also refracted (bent) slightly, just as light is bent when it passes through glass. Scientists study these changes to learn more about the structure of Earth.

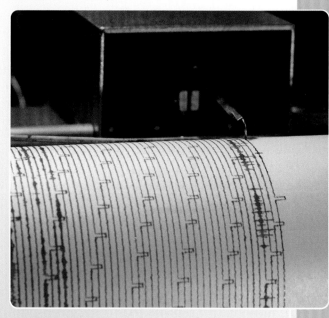

A seismograph records seismic wave vibrations as a series of wobbly lines on paper, as shown here, or on a computer monitor. By studying the speed, strength, and degree of refraction of the waves, scientists can figure out what kind of rocks the waves are passing through—whether they are solid or molten and their density (how much matter they contain per unit volume).

DATING ROCKS USING RADIOACTIVITY

Ernest Rutherford (1871–1937; right) and English geologist Arthur Holmes (1890–1965) discovered that some rocks contain radioactive particles that decay (break down) at a particular rate. This discovery was soon being used to date the rocks accurately, through a new technique called radiometric dating.

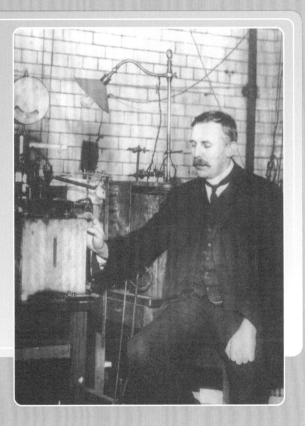

called seismic waves that pass through rocks during earthquakes. Milne founded seismology (the study of seismic waves). This has enabled scientists to study Earth's interior as well as the power of quakes. In the early 1900s Croatian scientist Andrija Mohorovičic (1857–1936) discovered the boundary between Earth's crust and the mantle using seismic waves.

In 1905 British physicist Ernest Rutherford (1871–1937) discovered a new and accurate method of dating rocks using radioactivity. This technique allowed scientists to begin to calculate the age of Earth itself. Geologists now believe the planet is much older than some nineteenth-century geologists believed—not millions, but 4.5 billion years old.

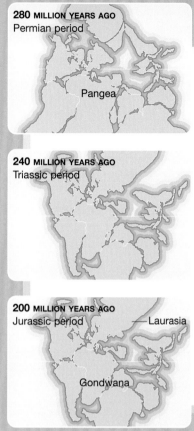

280 MILLION YEARS AGO
Permian period

Pangea

240 MILLION YEARS AGO
Triassic period

200 MILLION YEARS AGO
Jurassic period — Laurasia

Gondwana

140 MILLION YEARS AGO
Cretaceous period

PRESENT DAY
Quaternary period

EUROPE
Asia
North
America   Africa
South
America
Australia

*Present-day
coastlines are
white in all maps.*

DRIFTING CONTINENTS

Scientists now believe that Wegener was correct about continental drift: Earth's plates slowly drift on the underlying partly molten rocks. It is thought that the single supercontinent of Pangea began to break up about 200 million years ago. This formed two smaller but still vast continents: Laurasia in the north and Gondwana in the south. Around 135 million years ago, these also broke up to form the continents we know today, which very slowly drifted into their present positions. Wegener could not, however, explain why the continents move.

In 1912 a German scientist named Alfred Wegener came up with an extraordinary new theory: Continents, which geologists had always believed were fixed and immovable, drift very slowly across Earth's surface. Wegener thought that millions of years ago, Earth's land masses had been joined in a single, vast supercontinent he called Pangea, meaning "all-Earth." Later, Pangea broke up and eventually formed the continents as they exist today. The entire scientific world rejected Wegener's idea since it went against all the current theories about Earth's formation. More than fifty years passed before new discoveries showed that Wegener was right (see page 34).

Meanwhile, research into earthquakes and volcanoes continued. American seismologist Charles F. Richter and Italian earthquake expert Giuseppe Mercalli

MEASURING EARTHQUAKES

The scale devised by Charles F. Richter (1900–1985) measures the magnitude (size) of earthquakes in terms of the energy released. Each whole point on the Richter scale (below) represents a ten-fold increase in size and a more than thirty-fold increase in the amount of energy released. The Richter scale is not used to express earthquake damage. The twelve-point scale devised by Giuseppe Mercalli (1850–1914) measures the destructive power of earthquakes by assessing the damage they cause.

Richter Magnitudes	Earthquake Effects
Less than 3.5	Microearthquake; usually not felt but recorded.
3.5 to 5.4	Often felt but does not usually cause any damage.
Under 6.0	Perhaps slight damage to properly constructed buildings; can cause major damage to badly constructed buildings in some regions.
6.1 to 6.9	Can be destructive in areas up to 62 miles (100 km) across.
7.0 to 7.9	Major earthquake—can cause serious damage over large areas.
8 or more	Great earthquake—can cause serious damage in areas several hundred km across.

devised two scales to measure earthquakes. In the 1950s the launch of the first space satellites allowed scientists to see Earth's shape for the first time. It is round, and as Isaac Newton predicted two hundred and fifty years earlier, it bulges at the equator and flattens at the poles.

EVIDENCE FOR CONTINENTAL DRIFT

German meteorologist Alfred Wegener (1880–1930) used several kinds of evidence to support his theory, including the centuries-old observation that continents such as South America and Africa appeared as if they could fit together. The discovery of identical plant and animal fossils on continents now separated by vast oceans provided further clues. Wegener himself found fossils of tropical ferns on the Arctic island of Spitzbergen, which suggested that the island had once been located much farther south in a hotter region nearer the equator.

6 FUTURE PROSPECTS

The twentieth century saw the first evidence for continental drift and the idea that the seafloor spreads. The modern theory of plate tectonics combined these two theories and explained many of Earth's features for the first time.

IN THE 1950s BRITISH SCIENTIST Stanley K. Runcorn (1922–1995) and others provided evidence to support continental drift. Igneous rocks contain tiny magnetic minerals that line up with Earth's magnetic field as it was when the rocks formed. Younger rocks line up best with the current magnetic pole; older rocks do not. Runcorn figured that since the magnetic poles do not move much, the land masses must have moved across Earth's surface.

MID-OCEAN RIDGE AND SEAFLOOR SPREADING

Maurice Ewing and his colleagues discovered a valley that ran down the center of the mid-ocean ridge in the Atlantic. Earthquakes were common there. A little later, English scientists Frederick Vine (b. 1939) and Drummond Matthews (1931–1997) found alternating bands of magnetism in rocks on either side of the ridge. The pattern of banding was symmetrical on either side of the ridge, and the youngest rocks were nearer to the ridge. Rock samples taken from the seafloor by the drilling ship *Glomar Challenger* in the 1960s gave the same results. Based on such discoveries, Harry Hess suggested that molten rock welled up from the mid-ocean ridge, creating new seafloor when it cooled and hardened. This new seafloor gradually pushes the existing seafloor to the ocean's edges. That is why the rocks at the edges of the ocean floor are older than those at the center and why the bands of magnetism are symmetrical. The continents bordering the Atlantic Ocean are moving away from the Mid-Atlantic Ridge at a rate of 0.4–0.8 inch (1–2 cm) each year.

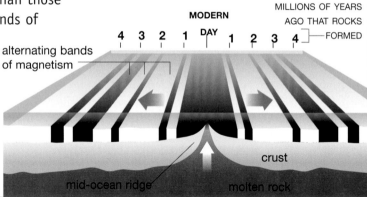

alternating bands of magnetism

4 3 2 1 **DAY** 1 2 3 4

MODERN

MILLIONS OF YEARS AGO THAT ROCKS FORMED

crust

mid-ocean ridge

molten rock

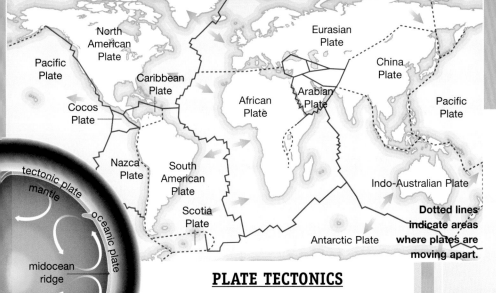

North
American
Plate

Pacific
Plate

Caribbean
Plate

Cocos
Plate

Eurasian
Plate

China
Plate

African
Plate

Arabian
Plate

Pacific
Plate

Nazca
Plate

South
American
Plate

Scotia
Plate

Indo-Australian Plate

**Dotted lines
indicate areas
where plates are
moving apart.**

Antarctic Plate

tectonic plate

mantle

oceanic plate

midocean
ridge

ocean
trench

continental plate

PLATE TECTONICS

The theory of plate tectonics states that Earth's crust is made up of about twenty plates that fit together like pieces in a giant jigsaw (above). The plates slowly push against one another, grind together, or pull apart. This activity causes volcanic activity and earthquakes. The plates of younger oceanic crust are thinner than those carrying older continents. Oceanic plates slide beneath continental plates where the two meet, forming deep gashes (ocean trenches). Mid-ocean ridges form where oceanic plates meet underwater.

Slow-churning currents of molten and partly molten rocks in the mantle (above left) cause tectonic plates to move. Rocks cycle up from mid-ocean ridges, out to the oceans' edges, and back into the mantle at ocean trenches.

MOUNTAINS

The theory of plate tectonics helps explain how fold mountains and volcanoes are formed. Fold mountains form where colliding plates cause rocks to crumple upward. Chains of volcanic mountains form near the edges of continents as oceanic crusts are forced down at ocean trenches. Deep inside, the crustal rocks melt to erupt again on land. Block mountains result when whole blocks of land are forced upward between cracks in Earth's crust. These cracks are called faults.

American scientist Maurice Ewing (1906–1974) found that on and next to the mid-ocean ridge the Atlantic seafloor rocks are young but get older the farther from the ridge they are. Geologist Harry Hess (1906–1969) suggested that this difference in age was caused by the seafloor spreading. By 1970, a group of American scientists combined the theories of continental drift and seafloor spreading in the plate tectonics model. It helped explain many different Earth processes, including how mountains form.

WHY EARTHQUAKES HAPPEN

Earthquakes commonly occur along ocean trenches or cracks in the land called faults, which occur at some plate boundaries. As the rocks there slowly grind against each other, the pressure builds up and up. Finally, the rocks shatter, which releases energy in the form of shock, or seismic, waves. The vibrations spread out through Earth from the focus (epicenter) of the earthquake, which may lie deep underground or nearer the surface.

Plate tectonics also explains why earthquakes occur along the border of plates, where rocks grind together. Volcanoes are common in the same zones for similar reasons. In addition, sensitive seismographs revealed more about Earth's interior. In the late 1970s explorers in deep-sea submersibles

EARTH'S INTERIOR

In the 1970s seismic reflective profiling showed geologists that Earth's crust was more complex than once thought. Scientists bounce sound waves from controlled underground explosions or electric vibrators between seismic detectors. The angle of refraction (bending) or reflection and the strength and speed of the waves reveal the structure of parts of the crust. The make up of layers beneath the crust were determined by studies of seismic waves created by large earthquakes. The mantle lies beneath the crust. It is about 1,860 miles (3,000 km) thick. Scientists now divide the mantle into three layers: a brittle upper layer called the lithosphere (**1**), which merges with the crust (**2**), a partly molten middle layer called the asthenosphere (**3**), and a molten lower layer called the mesosphere (**4**). Seismic testing has shown that the crust below the oceans, from zero to 4 miles (6 km) thick, is thinner than that below the continents, where it is 15–55 miles (25–90 km) thick. The dense core (**5**) is part solid, part liquid. It is made mostly of iron and nickel and reaches 4,500 °F (8,000 °C).

(small underwater craft) discovered vents called black smokers in mid-ocean ridges, where volcanic springs erupt clouds of hot, mineral-rich water. These hydrothermal ("hot water") vents form where Earth's crust is so thin that water can circulate deep into the crust, where it is heated. The vents teem with microbial life, and scientists believe these sites may be where life first began on Earth.

In recent years the study of earthquakes has been revolutionized by the development of ultrasensitive equipment, including lasers. People can now measure tiny shifts in the positions of rocks along faults or pick up the smallest tremors. Satellites are widely used by geologists to chart weather patterns and climate change, and map ocean currents, continents, ocean basins, and earthquake activity. Information gathered by modern instruments is fed into computers that can analyze the data in seconds. Computers are also used to predict all manner of Earth processes, from daily weather patterns to the likelihood of volcanic eruptions and earthquakes.

SATELLITE MEASUREMENTS

Satellites carry devices such as the Hubble space telescope (right). Measurements taken simultaneously from satellites orbiting above different points on Earth's surface have produced new, precise information about Earth's structure. For example, Earth is 27 miles (43 km) wider at the equator than it is "tall" from pole to pole. That means the planet is not a perfect sphere, but a slightly flattened, tangerine-like shape called a geoid.

BIOSPHERE IN A BOTTLE

GOALS
1. Create a mini-biosphere.
2. Observe ways in which organisms interact and sedimentation begins.

WHAT YOU WILL NEED

- clean quart jar (Mason jar) with a screw-top lid
- wax
- pond or lake water
- mud from a pond or lake
- water plants from an aquarium (such as *Elodea*)
- water snails

! SAFETY TIP
It is important for the wax valve to be put in the lid because a buildup of carbon dioxide gas could make the biosphere explode.

1 Ask an adult to make a hole in the lid with a nail. Cover the hole with a small piece of wax. It will act as a valve to release gases that might build up inside the jar.

2 Fill the jar ⅔ to ¾ full with pond water.

3 Add ½ to 1½ inches (1–4 cm) of mud from the pond bottom. At first the water will look murky—but the mud will settle at the bottom.

4 Add some *Elodea* or other small water plants.

5 Add some larger water plants and small pond-living creatures, such as snails. Do not add larger animals.

HANDY HINT

Be careful when you collect pond water. Only collect water from a shallow pond and use rubber gloves. Ask an adult to take you to a park if you do not have a pond. Do not remove too many organisms from the pond, or you could upset its natural balance.

SEDIMENTATION

The sediment at the bottom of the jar, and the animals and plants within it, is a mini-version of the bottom of a lake. You will be able to see the water clear as more mud settles at the bottom. Then you will see plants extend their roots into the mud, and tiny creatures make their homes in it. This is what happens at the beginning of the process of sedimentation. Over many thousands of years the mud will be turned into clay. And the animals and plants—when they die in and on it—will become fossils. Your experiment is the first stage.

6 Put the lid on the jar, and make careful observations of the contents over the next few weeks. Record the color of the water, the amount of light passing through, and the number of organisms that make their homes within the mud.

7 Watch over the next few weeks to see what happens in your biosphere, recording any changes that take place. After you are finished making observations, empty the contents of your biosphere into a nearby pond.

TIMELINE

Atoms and Molecules	**2500** BCE Tin ore is smelted in Turkey **200** BCE In South America people use furnaces to produce alloys (mixtures) of gold and silver	**1450** European metalworkers work out how to separate lead and silver ores
Electricity	**271** CE The compass is first used in China; it works by detecting Earth's magnetic field	**1180** The first reference to the magnetic compass in Western writing is in Alexander Neckam's *Concerning Natural Things (De Naturis Rerum)*
Evolution		
Genetics		
Geology	**500** BCE Xenophanes of Colphon (Greece) discovers that land can rise when he finds fossils of seashells on mountaintops	**1517** The Italian scientist Girolamo Fracastoro suggests that fossils are the remains of long-dead plants and animals
Gravity	**1450** BCE Egyptians devise a water clock, based on the principle of dripping water **330** BCE Aristotle believes that the Sun and planets orbit Earth	**1345** Dutch engineers use windmills to pump water out of areas that are being reclaimed from the sea
Light	**6000** BCE People in Italy make mirrors from a rock called obsidian **1361** BCE Chinese astronomers record a solar eclipse	**1021** Arab mathematician Alhazen writes about the refraction of light **1304** Theodoric of Freibourg, a German scientist, works out how rainbows form
Medicine	**2500** BCE Chinese doctors begin using a pain-killing technique called acupuncture **1550** BCE Egyptians are using about 700 drugs and medications	**365** Mechanical cranks are used to set broken bones in Greece **850** An Arab physician writes about eye disorders and treatments
Context	**c.3500** BCE The wheel is invented in Mesopotamia **2630** BCE Egyptians begin building the pyramids **776** BCE The first Olympic Games are held in Greece **117** CE Roman Empire reaches its greatest extent	**c.900** Mayan civilization in Mesoamerica collapses **1453** The Byzantine age comes to an end with the fall of Constantinople

5000 BCE   **300** CE

1709 A model hot-air balloon is made in Brazil **1714** Gabriel Fahrenheit constructs a mercury thermometer	**1738** Daniel Bernoulli proposes a kinetic theory of gases **c.1787** French physicist Jacques Charles draws up Charles's Law of gas volumes	
1701 Edmond Halley draws up a map of Earth's magnetic field **1729** Stephen Gray explains electrical conductors and insulators	**1742** Benjamin Franklin demonstrates the electrical nature of lightning **1800** Alessandro Volta develops the voltaic pile electric battery	**1807** Humphry Davy uses electrolysis to isolate potassium and sodium **1822** André-Marie Ampere works out the laws of the movement of electricity
		1809 Lamarck wrongly states that characteristics acquired during life are inherited by offspring **1831–36** Charles Darwin on HMS *Beagle*
	1760s Robert Bakewell improves farmstock by selectively breeding animals	**1831** Robert Brown is the first scientist to describe a cell nucleus
1691 Naturalist John Ray believes fossils are ancient life-forms	**1793** Mammoth remains are found in Siberian permafrost	**1811** Schoolgirl Mary Anning discovers the first fossil ichthyosaur **1815** Eruption of Mount Tambora in Indonesia modifies climates worldwide
1609 Johannes Kepler draws up laws of planetary motion **c.1665** Isaac Newton formulates his law of gravity		
1608 Hans Lippershey makes a refracting telescope with two lenses **1684** Street lighting is installed in parts of London	**1665** Robert Hooke proposes that light travels in waves **1671** Isaac Newton finds that a prism splits light into a spectrum of colors	**1811** William Wollaston invents the camera lucida **1839** Louis Daguerre invents a kind of photograph taken on metal plates
1628 Physician William Harvey explains the circulation of blood **1721** Smallpox inoculation is carried out in North America	**1745** Jacques Daviel successfully removes a cataract from a patient's eye	**1805** Japanese physician Seishu Hoanoka performs surgery with general anesthesia **1811** Charles Bell pioneers study of the nervous system
1630 English Puritans colonize Massachusetts Bay **1665** Bubonic plague kills one-fifth of London's population	**1787** The United States Constitution is adopted **1789** The French Revolution begins with the storming of the Bastille	**1803** The Louisiana Purchase doubles the size of the United States **1833** A law is passed in Britain to abolish slavery in the British Empire

1600   1730   1800   1850

TIMELINE

	1850	1900
Atoms and Molecules	**1892** James Dewar invents the vacuum bottle **1896** Henri Becquerel discovers radioactivity **1897** Physicist J.J. Thompson identifies electrons	**1905** Albert Einstein publishes his special theory of relativity **1910** The existence of the nucleus of an atom is proven by Ernest Rutherford
Electricity	**1877** American engineer Thomas Edison, invents the phonograph **1885** American electrical engineer William Stanley makes the first transformer	**1923** John Logie Baird makes a type of television
Evolution	**1856** Male Neanderthal skeleton found; it differs in important ways from modern human skeletons **1859** Charles Darwin publishes *On the Origin of Species*, arguing his case for evolution	**1908** Marcellin Boule reconstructs a skeleton of a Neanderthal person **1926** Hermann Muller creates genetic mutations in fruit flies, using X-rays
Genetics	**1865** Gregor Mendel, an Austrian monk, puts forward his laws of inheritance; they are published the following year	**1909** Danish botanist Wilhelm Johannsen defines a gene **1913** Chromosome mapping is pioneered by Alfred Sturtevant
Geology	**1860** The first fossil *Archaeopteryx* is found **1883** Mount Krakatoa, in Indonesia, erupts; it is one of the largest volcanic eruptions in recorded history	**1913** Earth's age is calculated at 4.6 billion years by Arthur Holmes **1935** Richter scale proposed to measure earthquake intensity
Gravity	**1851** Léon Foucault builds a pendulum that shows Earth's rotation. It is called Foucault's pendulum. **1891** John Poynting, an English physicist, works out the value of the gravitational constant	**1927** Georges Lemaitre suggests the universe originated with a "big bang"
Light	**1877** Joseph Swan, an English physicist, develops the first electric light bulb **1882** Albert Michelson calculates the speed of light to within 0.02 percent of the correct value	**1905** Albert Einstein publishes his special theory of relativity **1935** Transparency film invented by American photographers
Medicine	**1885** Louis Pasteur manufactures a rabies vaccine **1898** The cause of malaria, the protozoa *Plasmodium*, is discovered by physician Ronald Ross **1903** X-rays first used to treat cancerous tumors	**1929** Hormone estrogen first isolated **1934** Radio waves used to treat cancer **1943** Kidney dialysis machine built by Willem Kolff
Context	**1861–1865** American Civil War **1876** The Sioux Army of Sitting Bull defeats U.S. forces at the Battle of Little Bighorn **1897** The Klondike Gold Rush begins	**1901** Guglielmo Marconi makes the first transatlantic radio broadcast **1914–1918** World War I **1939–1945** World War II

1952 First hydrogen bomb is exploded
1960 First optical identification of a quasar
1967 Domestic microwave ovens are sold in U.S.

1994 American scientists discover a subatomic particle that they call the top quark
2004 A "supersolid" is discovered by American scientists—it flows through another material without friction

1961 The first silicon chips are manufactured
1962 The first national live TV transmission, a speech by President Truman in San Francisco
1975 First commercial personal computers sold

1990 Work begins on developing the World Wide Web
2007 American scientists create flexible batteries by weaving microscopic tubes of carbon into paper

1960 Remains of human ancestor *Homo habilis* discovered in Tanzania
1983 Fossils of a 16-million-year-old ancester of humans are found by Meave Leakey in Africa

1993 The oldest-known human ancestor, *Ardipithecus ramidus*, is discovered by Berkeley scientists
2003 Footprints of an upright-walking human, who was alive 350,000 years ago, are found in Italy

1953 The structure of DNA is discovered by Francis Crick and James Watson
1959 Down syndrome discovered to be caused by an extra chromosome

1994 The first genetically modifed tomato is sold in the U.S.
1996 A sheep named Dolly is cloned in Edinburgh
1998 Human stem cells are grown in a laboratory
2000 Human genome is roughly mapped out

1977 Frozen body of a baby mammoth found in Siberian permafrost

1996 Signs of microscopic life are found in a meteorite that originated from Mars
1997 Fossils of *Protarchaeopteryx*, a birdlike reptile, are found
2000 The fossil remains of a dinosaur's heart are found

1957 The first satelllites, Sputnik 1 and Sputnik 2, are sent into orbit around Earth by the Soviet Union

1992 Scientists at the University of Pisa, Italy, make the most accurate calculation of the acceleration due to gravity

1955 Indian scientist Narinder Kapany invents optical fibers for carrying light long distances
1962 Light-emitting diode (LED) invented

1998 Lasers are first used by American dentists for drilling teeth
2005 Flashes of light are discovered to create X-rays

1950 Link between smoking and lung cancer found
1958 Ultrasound scans are introduced to examine unborn babies
1967 The first successful heart transplant

1983 The human immunodeficiency virus (HIV) is discovered
1987 The first heart-lung-liver transplant is carried out by a team of British surgeons
2000 Works begins on making the first artificial heart

1955–1975 Vietnam War
1968 Martin Luther King assassinated in Memphis
1969 Neil Armstrong and Buzz Aldrin are the first people to walk on the Moon's surface

1989 Communist regimes across Europe collapse
1997 Diana, Princess of Wales, killed in a car accident in Paris
2001 Attack on the World Trade Center in New York
2008 Barack Obama elected first African-American president of U.S.

1950   **1990**   **2010**

KEY PEOPLE

Louis Agassiz (1807–1873)

Agassiz was born and grew up in Switzerland, but he later moved to the United States where he became a professor at Harvard University. He was the first person to outline the evidence that Earth has experienced an ice age. He researched the movement of glaciers and the debris that they leave behind. This debris is left long after the glacier ice has retreated and shows that Earth has been much colder in the past.

Aristotle (384–322 BCE)

Aristotle was born in Stagira, Greece, the son of a physician. When he was 17 he went to study at the Academy in Athens, which was then the greatest seat of learning in the world, before founding his own school, the Lyceum. Aristotle's writings spanned all branches of human knowledge, from zoology to politics, and made a lasting impact on the thoughts and scientific discoveries of later civilizations. In *A History of Animals* and *On the Generation of Animals,* he described the characteristics of different animal species and attempted to explain their behavior.

Nicolaus Copernicus (1473–1543)

Born in what is now Poland, the youngest of four children, Copernicus had many interests. One of the chief among them was astronomy, and he spent many hours studying the night sky. Some of his observations made him doubt the accepted belief that Earth was the center of the universe. Shortly before his death, Copernicus published *On the Revolutions of the Celestial Spheres*, in which he argued that the Sun was the center of the universe. The theory was called heliocentrism.

Alexander von Humboldt (1769–1859)

German explorer and naturalist Humboldt traveled extensively, especially in the Caribbean and South America. He made many natural history discoveries and was once a guest of President Thomas Jefferson in the White House. He discovered that many rocks once thought to have been the product of a great flood were actually igneous in origin, so damaging the incorrect ideas of the Neptunists. Humboldt also made the discovery that similar rocks were present on the coasts of eastern South America and western Africa, supporting the idea that the two continents had once been joined. He has a penguin, a squid, a skunk, several mountains, an ocean current, and a river named for him.

James Hutton (1726–1797)

Hutton was born in Edinburgh, and went on to become a farmer, physician, and keen amateur geologist who developed the "principle of uniformitarianism." This theory argued that current geological processes—the erosive work of waves, the deposition that takes places in lakes, the cutting of river valleys, and so on— are the same as those that worked on Earth's surface in the distant past. Hutton drew the conclusion from this that Earth must be very much older than previously thought. His book *The Theory of the Earth*, published in 1790, expanded on this idea.

Leonardo da Vinci (1452–1519)

Leonardo was born in Vinci, Italy, and was apprenticed to a sculptor and painter at the age of 16. Throughout his life he designed and sketched machines ranging from pulleys to pumps, and from flying machines to submarines. He also said that fossils of shells found on mountains had once been animals living in the ocean. Many of his notes and sketches have been lost but 7,000 pages survive.

Gerardus Mercator (1512–1594)

Born Gerhard Kremer in Flanders, Mercator changed his name when he went to university in

1530. He developed an interest in astronomy, geography, math, and art. As a young man he made maps and globes, and in 1569, at the age of 57, he drew his Great World Map, which covered the whole of the world as it was then known. This was enormously useful for explorers and traders alike.

Isaac Newton (1643–1727)

Newton was an English physicist and mathematician. He was the greatest scientist of his era and one of the most influential in history. Newton became very interested in astronomy while at Cambridge University and eventually discovered that Earth's rotation caused it to bulge slightly at the equator and flatten at the poles. It was only in the 1960s that satellite photographs from space confirmed this. In 1687, with his friend Edmond Halley, Newton showed how a universal force—gravity—applies to all objects in the universe.

Pliny the Elder (23–79)

Pliny the Elder was a Roman author, naturalist, and philosopher, as well as a naval and army commander in the early Roman Empire. The *Naturalis Historia*, published probably in 79, is one of the largest single works to have survived from the Roman empire to the modern day. It covers most of what the Romans knew about science.

Pythagoras (c. 580–500 BCE)

Pythagoras is thought to have been born on the Greek island of Samos. He was a philosopher and founded a school of ideas called the Pythagoreans. He is best known for his contributions to math.

Charles Richter (1900–1985)

Born in Hamilton, Ohio, Richter studied at Stanford University and the California Institute of Technology. With coworker Beno Gutenberg

he devised a scale for measuring the relative strength of earthquakes. Later, he helped develop construction codes to ensure that buildings in earthquake-prone areas were as safe as possible. Agassiz's warnings were credited with saving many lives in the 1971 Los Angeles earthquake.

William Smith (1769–1839)

Smith was the son of an English blacksmith who went on to become one of the pioneers of geology. He produced the first geological maps but was often not given the credit he was due and was often poor. He was even jailed for two years when he became bankrupt. Smith recognized that rock strata of different ages contained distinct combinations of fossils, so rocks of a similar age could be matched across regions by comparing their fossils. A crater on the planet Mars is named for him.

Thales of Miletus (625–546 BCE)

The philosopher Thales was the first of the ancient Greeks to attempt to explain natural phenomena without reference to mythology. He advanced people's understanding of geometry, was the first to study electricity, and tried to work out the nature of matter.

Alfred Wegener (1880–1930)

Wegener was born in Berlin, Germany. Among his achievements were several discoveries about the weather and a record-breaking hot-air balloon flight of 52 hours. However, his greatest claim to fame was his theory of "continental drift," which he put forward in 1912. Wegener argued that the continents had moved around Earth's surface over the course of many millions of years. Sometimes they had joined together, and at other times they had separated. This idea—now called plate tectonics—was not generally accepted until the 1960s. He died on an expedition to Greenland.

GLOSSARY

axis An imaginary line that runs between the North and South Poles, about which Earth spins.

black smoker A vent or hot spring found in volcanically active parts of the seafloor, which emits clouds of hot, dark, mineral-rich water.

circumference The outer edge of a circle, also the distance around Earth.

continental drift The theory that the continents are not fixed but slowly drift across Earth's surface.

continental shelf Submerged border of a land mass.

crust The outer, surface layer of Earth.

earthquake Shock waves generated by tectonic movement in Earth's crust or mantle.

fault A crack in the rocks, often near the edges of tectonic plates. Earthquakes commonly occur along faults.

fossil The remains of plants or animals that have been preserved in stone.

geology The study of the rocks that form the planet, and also of Earth's structure and formation.

glaciation Processes by which the landscape is molded by the erosive action of glaciers.

Ice Age A period when Earth's climate was considerably cooler than it is now, when ice sheets covered large parts of Earth's dry land.

igneous rock Rock that formed when molten rock erupted by volcanoes cools at the surface.

magnetosphere Earth's magnetic field, which helps protect the planet from solar radiation.

mantle The thick layer of hot, semisolid rock that lies inside Earth between the crust and the core.

metamorphic rock Rock that has been transformed from existing rock through great heat or pressure.

meteorite Meteor fragment consisting of stone or iron that passes through Earth's atmosphere and reaches the ground intact.

midocean ridge Submarine ridge marking the boundary between two tectonic plates.

moraine The sediment carried along by a glacier and later deposited along its borders.

paleontology The study of fossils.

planet A heavenly body such as Mars, Jupiter, or Earth that revolves around the Sun or another star.

plate tectonics The theory that Earth's crust is made up of twenty or so giant plates that are constantly, but slowly, in motion.

Richter scale Scale used to express the amount of energy released by earthquakes.

sediment Rock debris such as sand, silt, gravel, or mud.

sedimentary rock Rock formed from layers of sediment that were later compressed (squashed).

seismic belt Area of Earth's surface particularly prone to earthquakes.

seismic waves Shock waves or vibrations that pass through the ground, caused by earthquakes or explosions.

seismology The study of earthquakes and Earth's structure using seismic (shock) waves.

seismometer An instrument that measures earthquakes.

strata Layers of sedimentary rock.

superposition The theory that rocks are laid down in horizontal layers called strata, with the oldest layers at the bottom and younger layers on top.

tectonic plate One of the huge, rigid plates that make up the outer layer (crust) of Earth. Earth's tectonic plates are constantly moving.

FOR MORE INFORMATION

BOOKS

Blashfield, Jean. *When Land, Sea, and Life Began*. Chicago, IL: Heinemann Library, 2006.

Brown, Cynthia. *Explore Rocks and Minerals!* White River Junction, VT: Nomad, 2010.

Colson, Mary. *Shaky Ground: Earthquakes*. Chicago, IL: Raintree, 2006.

Gardner, Robert. *Earth-shaking Science Projects about Planet Earth*. Berkely Heights, NJ: Enslow, 2008.

Marshak, Stephen. *Essentials of Geology: Portrait of Earth*. New York: W.W. Norton, 2009.

Naish, Darren. *The Great Dinosaur Discoveries*. Berkeley, CA: University of California Press, 2009.

Pluckrose, Henry. *Earth*. North Mankato, MN: Sea to Sea Publications, 2007.

Prothero, Donald R., and Robert Dott. *Evolution of the Earth*. New York: McGraw-Hill Science, 2003.

Various. *Forces of Nature*. Chicago, IL: World Book, 2009.

WEB SITES

Due to the changing nature of Internet links, Rosen Publishing has developed an online list of Web sites related to the subject of this book. This site is updated regularly. Please use this link to access the list:

http://www.rosenlinks.com/scipa/geo

INDEX